The Culper Ring

A Captivating Guide to George Washington's Spy Ring and its Impact on the American Revolution

Free Bonus from Captivating History (Available for a Limited time)

Hi History Lovers!

Now you have a chance to join our exclusive history list so you can get your first history ebook for free as well as discounts and a potential to get more history books for free! Simply visit the link below to join.

Captivatinghistory.com/ebook

Also, make sure to follow us on:

Twitter: @Captivhistory

Facebook: Captivating History:@captivatinghistory

Contents

Introduction – The Secret Side of War

Spying and warfare have always gone hand-in-hand. From Julius Caesar to modern generals, we have accounts of commanders covertly gathering information about their opponents, ensuring they have the intelligence they need to conduct a war.

Because of the nature of their work, the stories of spies are often lost to history. Those operating in the ancient world, when documentary evidence was slim, seldom left any trails. In more recent times, there have often been reasons to deliberately hide the trail. It is probably no coincidence that 85% of the records for the Special Operations Executive, Britain's covert operations organisation of the Second World War, were destroyed in a mysterious fire. Even after their work is done, the revelation of a spy's identity can be dangerous, while sharing techniques can lose a nation its edge.

It is hardly surprising the work of spies during the American Revolution remain shrouded in secrecy. Though their work was vital to the cause of freedom, it was carried out in the shadows, often informally, and with a great deal of care for secrecy. Anyone caught spying was liable to be hanged by the British.

This was a war in which it was relatively easy to put spies into the field. The two sides shared a common language and culture. Loyalties were divided, and some men could as easily have taken the British side as the revolutionary one. Spies didn't have to be picked out for specialist language skills. It was easy for them to blend in and to understand documents they obtained or conversations they overheard. The lives of the two sides were already deeply entangled.

Some of these spies were celebrated during their lifetimes. The achievements of others remained concealed. During the 20th century, hidden parts of their story were gradually revealed. Historians pieced together the fragments of information available, joining the dots to turn isolated incidents into a picture of these men at work. By comparing documents and identifying handwriting, they discovered spies whose identities had remained secret for more than a century. The activities of the agents working for Washington and other revolutionary commanders were revealed, though much remains unknown, including how deeply some of the minor players were involved.

Foremost among these spies were the agents of the Culper Ring. Based in New York during the British occupation, they provided vital intelligence from behind enemy lines. Their work gave Washington an insight into the British forces and their plans. They helped to turn the war in the revolutionaries' favour. And now their story can be told once more.

Chapter One: Before the Culper Ring

The Early War

By the summer of 1776, progress in the Revolutionary War had turned against the cause of independence.

The war had started well for the revolutionaries. Every colony had joined together to gain independence from Britain. The British spent a lot of lives and resources in an attempt to seize the Charlestown peninsula, only to give up on efforts to relieve a besieged Boston, withdrawing from the region. A raid on Fort Ticonderoga had supplied the Americans with artillery, with which they began a bombardment of Boston.

Further south, attempts by the royal governor Lord Dunmore to suppress the revolution in Virginia had failed. He was defeated in battle at Great Bridge and retreated to Norfolk, before fleeing by sea. In South Carolina, a conflict between Loyalist and Patriot militias saw the Loyalists driven out of the colony over the winter of 1775-6.

But not everything was going the Patriots' way, and soon the tide of war threatened to turn. In Britain, the government recognised the need to recruit more men and send them to fight for the colonies. They took the unusual step of arming Irish Catholics as part of this force, recognising that Irish Protestants were more sympathetic to the Presbyterian-dominated revolutionaries and their cause.

In the north, the Patriots tried to raise a Canadian revolution against the British, calling upon natives and French-speaking Quebecois to join their cause. But a campaign launched against Quebec failed and the Patriot forces retreated.

In the summer of 1776, William Howe, one of the leading British generals, went on the offensive. He landed troops on Staten Island and defeated Washington in the Battle of Long Island. By September, the Patriots were in retreat, leaving Howe to take control of New York, the most important trading port in America and already one of the leading cities in the world.

As Washington prepared to retreat from New York, the Patriot leadership faced a difficult decision - one that would provide both the necessity and the opportunity to create the Culper Ring.

New York was a beautiful city and a great trading port. If they left it standing, it would give shelter to the British army. Many merchants in the town would inevitably help to supply the British army with food, whether because of Loyalist sympathies or because they chose profit over patriotism. The British military, better organised, equipped, and experienced than its militia opponents, would be almost impossible to dislodge once it was established in the city. Many urged Washington to burn New York down before he left.

But destroying New York had huge disadvantages. It would displace tens of thousands of people. It would turn many New Yorkers against the Patriot cause. And in the long term, it would deprive a newly established nation of one of its most significant assets.

Rather than choose between these two abysmal options, Washington passed the decision to Congress. They ordered him not to burn New York. The city was left for Howe to take.

And so, the stage was set for the most important web of espionage in the Revolutionary War. Washington needed to gain every advantage he could if he was to beat the British. New York, the headquarters of Howe's army, the center of British supply lines, and home to thousands of sympathetic Patriots, was the perfect place for spies to operate. The operations that would precede the Culper Ring were about to begin.

First Steps in Espionage

Howe's offensive against New York was the scene of some limited espionage by Washington and his officers. Generals Mercer and Livingston both succeeded in sneaking spies into occupied territory to find out about British forces and movements, and one of these men overheard conversations between British generals. But the information provided was limited and inaccurate, indicating an impending attack on New Jersey when the real target was Long Island.

As the pressure mounted, so did the espionage efforts. Governor George Clinton hatched a scheme to kidnap and question two Tories, but this came to nothing. He also snuck two Patriot agents, Benjamin Ludlum and William Treadwell, into British-occupied Long Island, but they returned with inaccurate troop numbers and vague, useless insights.

Part of the problem was Washington was limiting himself in his aims and methods. Instead of trying to place long-term agents behind enemy lines, he was sending one- or two-man scouting parties to observe the enemy, often under cover of night, and gain military intelligence - information on the positions and movements of troops. It was the sort of intelligence work Washington had done during the French and Indian War, and which in Europe was regarded as a suitable activity for an officer and a gentleman. There was little training or support for this work, and no expertise available in real spycraft.

A Telling Fiasco: Hale Versus Rogers

Born in Coventry, Connecticut, in 1755, Nathan Hale was a native-born son of the colonies. The sixth child of a strict Congregationalist family, he was assiduous in his daily prayers and had been educated for a career in the church. In 1769 he went to Yale, which at the time was home to around a hundred students, where the atmosphere of discipline and strict religious observance matched his old life at home.

The curriculum at Yale was grounded in the obsessions of the European Enlightenment, which in turn had evolved from Medieval and ancient thinking. It included ancient languages, logic, rhetoric, and mathematics, subjects which would help to sharpen the mind in a variety of different ways. But more useful for a future spy were the intellectual activities students engaged in during their free time. Hale was a member of the Linonia debating society, the Brothers in Unity literary society, and took part in theatrical productions including Robert Dodsley's *The Toy Shop*. Such activities gave him skills in acting and in fast talking that he would use later.

Hale's time at Yale was not all productive. He began to enjoy the life of a young man, drinking and misbehaving, often in the company of his classmate Benjamin Tallmadge, the future head of the Culper Ring. Only three months after he arrived at Yale, Hale's father wrote to him urging him to focus onhis studies.

Yale formed Hale in other ways. It was a hotbed of radicalism which the Loyalist Thomas Jones labelled "a nursery of sedition." Its students were the first in America to boycott British goods in protest at the events leading up to the revolution. This was a place that helped to cement Hale's Patriot tendencies.

By the time he graduated, Hale had decided against the life of ministry his family had planned for him. Instead, he became a schoolmaster. His first job was in a Connecticut town whose quiet atmosphere bored him. In less than a year he was applying for another job.

When the war came, it offered an opportunity for excitement as well as the chance to fulfill his patriotic duty. Hale signed up almost immediately, becoming a first lieutenant in the third company of the Seventh Regiment, a newly raised Connecticut militia unit. As 1776 approached, and the terms of enlistment came to an end, he was promoted to captain-lieutenant rather than leave alongside many of his peers. His regiment was retitled the Nineteenth Foot, as Washington reorganised his disparate militias into a single army of revolution.

Hale missed the engagements with Howe during the early stages of the war. He arrived outside Boston in time to join a period of relative peace and inactivity, during which he filled his time drinking, playing checkers, and writing poems. If he had been looking for excitement, this wasn't it, but it was at least more fun than the life of a backwoods teacher.

In March 1776, Hale's unit was relocated to New York, as Washington prepared to face a British counter-attack. Hale was appalled by the attitude of many locals, who eagerly awaited the return of the British.

By late August, Hale had been moved to Brooklyn. Held in reserve, he and his comrades in arms bore witness to the American defeat there on the 27th and 28th and took part in the subsequent retreat.

Frustrated at the lack of action, Hale transferred to Knowlton's Rangers, a new unit led by Lieutenant Colonel Thomas Knowlton, which was being prepared for special scouting operations. This force offered the guarantee of action to the impetuous young Hale. By the start of September, Captain Hale was leading a company in reconnaissance operations.

Washington approached Knowlton and asked him to recruit men from his unit to act as spies. Knowlton had experience in this area, having helped General Mercer to get an agent onto Staten Island in July. But almost none of the officers in the Rangers wanted to be a spy. A task involving trickery and deception, it was regarded as beneath the dignity of a gentleman. In the end, the recruitment effort was saved from failure by one man, as Hale volunteered.

Hale was a distinctive looking young man, with handsome features, a large mole on his neck, and some scars on his forehead caused by a gunpowder flash - a hazard of using the era's black powder weapons. He wasn't going to blend in as easily as others might. But he was smart, brave, and willing to take on the task. For a commanding officer in desperate need of good intelligence, those were all the qualifications that mattered.

Washington met with Hale to provide him with instructions for his mission. Rather than taking the direct route of a military scout, landing in occupied Brooklyn or Staten Island, he would travel into Connecticut and then cross the Sound to land behind the British army. He would travel up Long Island, observing the troops and supplies being mustered there, their destinations, and when they began embarking on ships for the next stage of the British advance. It was a mission that would set the pattern for the Culper Ring's work, including the information gathered and the route used.

The war had made the Sound a haven for illicit activity, as smugglers and gun runners profited from selling to both sides. The British and Americans both had ships in the area to support their own activities and prevent smuggling to their opponents. These were dangerous waters.

A pair of Patriot ships, the Schuyler and the Montgomery, transported Hale across the Sound under cover of darkness on the night of the 16th of September. He was rowed ashore before dawn on the 17th, dressed in civilian clothes and with his only identifying document his diploma, which would allow him to claim he was a travelling teacher. He was ready to begin his work.

The Halifax, a British ship, came within hours of catching them during this perilous expedition. Even after missing the Patriot's vessels, the British were left wondering why they had approached the Long Island shore. One man on the Halifax, Robert Rogers, was particularly interested.

Rogers was a man with an eye for skullduggery. A veteran military scout and commander of a force of rangers, he had tried to play both sides off against each other to get himself the best possible position at the start of the war. He had even gone so far as to seek permission to travel as a civilian behind American lines, hiding the fact he was being paid by the British. This rightly drew suspicion from Washington, leading to Rogers' capture and escape from captivity. Few British soldiers were more duplicitous. Rogers' own experience in lies and deception would help him spot lies in others.

Rogers and his rangers were launching raids against the Patriots across the Long Island Sound, as well as interfering with enemy activities there. Rogers recruited agents up and down the coast, offering good payment for information, and so by the time Hale crossed the Sound, Rogers had heard about two British ships lurking suspiciously in the area. He and a band of Rangers took sail on the Halifax to intercept them, arriving too late. But another of Rogers' agents saw the Schuyler lurking in the port at Norwalk and a man being dropped off there. It was clear to Rogers thatthe Patriots had planted a spy behind Loyalist lines.

In the time it took Hale to get into position, the war had moved on. Howe had launched his big attack, making Hale's original mission redundant. He would have to advance further and more quickly if he was going to gather valuable information. As he rushed to catch up with the advancing armies, his lack of subtlety gave the game away.

Rogers, anticipating Hale's actions, had himself and his men dropped off ahead of the spy's route to the front. On the 19th, they spotted Hale. Rather than snatch him up, they spent the whole of the 20th covertly watching him as he took notes of every barracks and military unit he passed.

That evening, Rogers approached Hale in the tavern where he was spending the night. Pretending to be a Patriot militiaman trapped behind enemy lines, Rogers earned Hale's trust. Hale soon confessed who he was and what his mission was, believing he was recruiting Rogers to work with him. Rogers was now confident of his man but needed him to confess in front of witnesses. He invited Hale to join him for dinner at another tavern the next day.

On the afternoon of the 21st, Hale joined Rogers for dinner. With Rogers were several other men who he introduced as fellow Patriots, but who were rangers in disguise. While they drank, and Hale talked about his mission, others of Rogers' men surrounded the tavern. Hale was seized. As he was led outside in irons, several passers-by identified him as a member of the Connecticut Hale family and a rebel.

The Rangers took Hale to General Howe's headquarters. Arriving late at night, Rogers had Howe fetched from bed to sign a death warrant. The evidence against Hale included all the notes he had taken while spying and his confession in front of witnesses. A known enemy operative caught in plain clothes, he was condemned as a spy without the need for a full court-martial.

The next morning, Hale was taken to the artillery park. He delivered his last words, speaking with composure of how he had done his duty. He was hanged and buried there.

That evening, word reached the Patriot command of what had happened. They did not want to damage morale by letting word get out of the botched operation, and so Hale's name was quietly entered into the casualty records while nothing was publicly made of the incident. Behind closed doors, some were indignant at the execution of one of their own, seething for revenge.

Because of the cover-up, rumours of Hale's fate did not reach his family until the end of September. In late October, his brother Enoch finally obtained confirmation of what had happened, and he had to travel to the army camp himself in search of news. Hale's embarrassed superiors had done his family and his memory a disservice. But they would at least learn lessons from the disastrous mission that led to his death.

Clark and Tallmadge: Laying the Groundwork for Culper

As Washington withdrew from New York, the already difficult challenge of gathering good intelligence became nearly impossible. The advancing British could get information about Patriot forces from the people left behind in areas they passed through, but that was not an option for Washington. There were no longer refugees or illicit travellers reaching his camp from occupied territory. Without a permanent base, any agents he tried to plant would be unable to send messages or return to him. Even his military scouts were not penetrating as deeply toward the enemy as he wanted.

Despite the difficulties, Washington was unwilling to give up on intelligence work. He asked Colonel John Cadwalader to recruit agents not only to gather intelligence on the enemy but also to execute counterintelligence, spreading misinformation about American military activities. Late in December one of these agents procured a map of British deployments around Princeton, while also convincing some British officers the Americans had more soldiers than they did. Meanwhile, scouts for both sides snuck across enemy lines under cover of night, counting numbers and estimating dispositions.

The turn of the year brought a significant change. Following the Battles of Denton and Princeton, the British withdrew to New York. No longer preoccupied with retreat, Washington could sit still in the hills around Morristown, where he had time to seriously consider his intelligence-gathering efforts.

Washington recognised he needed to recruit civilians as spies, instead of the military men he had used previously. A middle-aged man named Nathaniel Sackett was hired to head up the operation. Employed on a salary of $50 a month, he was also given a budget of $500 to enter New York and recruit agents.

Sackett would need support - someone with military authority who could liaise with officers and order dispatch riders to carry intelligence to the general. For this, he was given a deputy - Captain Benjamin Tallmadge of the Second Continental Light Dragoons.

Like his best friend Nathaniel Hale, Tallmadge had gone from studying at Yale to become a teacher. Unlike Hale, his first teaching post suited him, as he got to socialise with the leading families of Wethersfield, Connecticut. There, he found himself among people of revolutionary tendency, who gradually won him around to cause. Though initially reticent, he became increasingly convinced the revolution was a religiously righteous cause. In June 1776, he signed up to fight. Again, his experience had parallels with Hale's, but without the frustrations. He was in Brooklyn in time to face the British advance, took part in the fighting instead of sitting it out, and withdrew with the rest of Washington's forces.

William Tallmadge, Benjamin's older brother, was captured by the British during the fighting and died soon after on a prison boat. Benjamin Tallmadge's commitment to the rebel cause had become personal.

Smart and well connected, Tallmadge was quickly promoted through the ranks. He first came to Washington's attention while acting as a brigade major for General Jeremiah Wadsworth in October. Two months later, he was offered a captain's post in the newly raised Second Dragoons, led by Colonel Elisha Sheldon. In this new role, he commanded a unit of 43 men trained to fight both on horse and on foot, whose job was to carry out scouting missions and skirmish with their opposite numbers on the British side.

Following their formation, the Second Dragoons travelled into Connecticut to buy their horses. While on this mundane purchasing mission, Tallmadge began his work as Sackett's military man, as Sackett started running his espionage work across Long Island Sound.

The first operation Tallmadge was involved in was a covert intelligence mission by Major John Clark. A young lawyer turned specialist military scout, Clark was smuggled onto Long Island with Tallmadge's help. There he learned to blend in with the locals and to covertly watch the British troops. He spent months behind enemy lines, gathering information on British forces and how the opposing army was run. Tallmadge had grown up in Setauket on Long Island, and it is likely his family and other contacts there helped to shelter Clark as well as to carry messages back across the Sound. Clark's intelligence, passed to Washington via Tallmadge and Sackett, provided valuable insight into what was happening among the enemy.

While Clark was on Long Island, Tallmadge was promoted to major, then summoned along with the rest of his regiment to join the army in New Jersey. There, the dragoons returned to their scouting and skirmishing role.

Meanwhile, Sackett was developing groundbreaking espionage

techniques that would become fundamental to American intelligence work. Instead of sending in temporary agents to gather specific information and come back out with it, he established permanent agents living in enemy territory under assumed personas. They provided him with intelligence reports on whatever was happening at the time, theoretically ensuring a steady supply of intelligence and greater security for the agents, whose identities Sackett was careful to protect.

Unfortunately, the quality of agents and their intelligence was less impressive than the quality of Sackett's work, and he was unable to provide as much intelligence as Washington wanted. Some mysterious fiasco befell his operations, apparently involving a horse and a doctor, though the details were sadly never recorded. In the aftermath, he was removed from Washington's intelligence operations, with a parting payment of $500.

Both sides were increasingly ruthless in tackling enemy sources of information. Spies and traitors were executed in growing numbers, including Loyalist recruiters caught by the Patriots. In an atmosphere of hostility and paranoia, a few misplaced words or a suspicious look at the wrong moment could get someone hanged.

Washington had learned some critical lessons in intelligence analysis from his work with Sackett. He realised that to be valuable information had to be received in a timely way, so it was still relevant. It also had to be cross-referenced, particularly where troop estimates were concerned, as agents made mistakes and a single report could not be relied upon when lives were at stake.

Sometime in the summer, Clark returned from his work on Long Island, in time to be wounded in a skirmish with the British.

In September, the British again defeated the Patriots, this time at Brandywine, allowing them to take Philadelphia. Washington, aware of Clark's excellent work, sent him out to establish a network of spies around the newly captured city and the forts defending it. The agent spent three months undercover, sleeping rough in the countryside, suffering from winter weather and pain from his injured shoulder. In that time, he sent 30 reports on enemy activity to Washington as well as planting false information through his contacts. Smugglers, allowed through the British lines due to a shortage of supplies, became some of his most useful agents. He also got messages through using a pile of official British passes he laid hands on.

But this could not continue. Clark's injury would not heal properly, and he was exhausted from months of gruelling field work. He missed his wife, who he hadn't seen in a year. A grateful Washington provided him with a contact who found him a desk job auditing the army's expenses. Major Clark's impressive career in espionage had come to an end.

That the reins would be taken up by Tallmadge was not immediately apparent. He had spent the rest of 1777 in scouting and skirmishing with the British, witnessing atrocities by the British cavalry that outraged him. Early in 1778, his regiment was given a chance to rest. But in taking their own time off, the officers failed to deal with the state of neglect their men and horses had fallen into. Tallmadge and the other officers were rebuked for their failings, and Washington, with whom he had previously had a positive relationship, froze the young major out.

In June, the tide of war shifted once more. The British, now led by Henry Clinton, realised they could not hold Philadelphia. They retreated to New York, harassed the whole way by Washington. By the end of the month, the Patriots once again sat facing British-occupied New York. They were going to need intelligence on what was happening inside.

Benjamin Tallmadge's hour had come.

Chapter Two: The Birth of the Culper Ring

A City Facing Both Ways

Despite Congress's decision to save the city, New York was devastated by fire just after the original British occupation in 1776. An accidental conflagration was encouraged by those who wanted to see the city burn, and though it was saved from totaldestruction by the demolition of buildings to form firebreaks, it became an ash-shrouded shell of its former glory.

In this atmosphere lived the desperate, the greedy, and the tenacious. Those profiting from the war held grand parties streets away from destitute refugees and tensely pacing redcoats. Smuggling was rife. Formerly smart districts were given over to prostitutes servicing the troops. Legitimate businesses continued to work, printing newspapers, selling groceries, serving food and drink to those who could afford it. But this was not the noble, independent-spirited city it had once been.

The city's inhabitants survived by being willing to look both ways. Whoever marched through their city and its surroundings, the crowds would cheer them on. Whoever was paying for information, someone would bring it to them. Whoever sought out supplies could buy them, for the right price. Though there were some in the city fiercely dedicated to each side, the overall atmosphere was of people just trying to get by. Loyalties were uncertain. Some were for sale, while others were carefully kept secrets, a burning dedication to a cause that their owners felt forced to keep quiet.

It was the perfect place for spies.

Brewster Begins

On the 7th of August, Washington received a letter from Lieutenant Caleb Brewster.

A former whaler from Norwalk, Brewster had grown up alongside Tallmadge in the Presbyterian community of Setauket, on the east side of Long Island. A man with a craving for adventure, he gave up farming at 19 to become a whaler, a job involving hard work, danger, and months of deprivation, but which brought with it action and the chance for significant profit thanks to the value of whale oil. When war broke out, he joined the Suffolk County militia, becoming a full lieutenant in early 1776. When his company disbanded, he stayed with the army and took part in successful boat-borne raids across Long Island Sound in the fall of 1776. He was part of the network Tallmadge used to support Clark on Long Island but spent most of 1777 and the first half of 1778 with the primary Patriot army.

Now Brewster offered to use his daring and local knowledge for a different sort of adventure. He wanted to be an agent for Washington, as Clark had been.

It was an opening Washington sorely needed. He knew nothing about what was happening with the British inside New York - not their numbers, not their commanders, not their movements. If he was to beat them, he needed a source of timely information. But he had been bitten before and was wary of fostering another unreliable source, as had happened with Hale and Sackett. So, he wrote back to Brewster setting out what he needed. The information had to be timely and specific to be useful. He specified the sort of information he wanted, including the movements of troops, numbers of draft horses, and supplies of provisions.

Brewster submitted his first report on the 27th of August. It detailed the return of British ships to New York harbour, damaged by storms and a fight against the French fleet. There was also information about where troops were being gathered in and around New York, which showed the British were preparing to relieve their garrison at Newport. This was vital intelligence for Washington, who did not know where the British fleet was, and who had been working on plans to seize Newport.

Brewster had proved his value and Washington intended to keep using him. Like Clark, Brewster would need a support structure within the Patriot military, someone who could provide a regular channel for messages to the general.

Washington chose General Charles Scott to oversee Brewster's work. Scott was an experienced soldier and a commander of light infantry, troops who specialised in scouting and skirmishing. He, therefore, had the right mindset and experience for information gathering work. His job would be not just to oversee the existing spy but to recruit more agents to work with him.

As Scott's aide in this, Washington chose Tallmadge. His dragoons regularly worked with the light infantry, he had experience from his work with Sackett and Clark, and he knew both Brewster and the local area.

As a general and field commander, Scott was already a busy man, so much of the intelligence work fell upon Tallmadge. After the shame of being reprimanded earlier in the year, this was his chance for redemption.

Woodhull Becomes Culper

One of Tallmadge's first recruits was a Long Island farmer named Abraham Woodhull, another man he had known from childhood. Woodhull had become involved in smuggling through his farm produce. He would take his goods to New York, where there was a shortage of basic foodstuffs, but a plentiful supply of the luxuries provided by Britain's international trade. He bartered produce for luxuries, then crossed the Sound to Patriot-controlled areas, where he sold these luxuries, hard to obtain in the revolutionary territory, for hard cash.

Most military men were happy to turn a blind eye to smuggling, but politicians were concerned that reminders of British luxuries might stoke loyalist sentiments, and so periodic attempts were made to stop the smugglers. Woodhull was captured in one of these efforts and ended up in a Connecticut jail.

In August 1778, Tallmadge arranged Woodhull's release. In return, Woodhull was recruited as an agent. Smugglers already brought small pieces of intelligence out of New York along with tea and silk. Woodhull's recruitment was the logical extension of this.

Woodhull was less drawn to the action than Tallmadge and Brewster and had long been more politically moderate than them. But in September 1777, his relative General Nathanial Woodhull died in British captivity, allegedly dying from mistreatment by his captors. The truth of his death remains uncertain, but Woodhull bought into the dark narrative of unjustified assault printed in the Patriot press. He became fervently anti-British. When Tallmadge offered him the chance to serve the revolution, it was also Woodhull's chance to pursue a personal vendetta. Woodhull was more than happy to sign up, taking on a task that would let him carry on providing for his family while he struck back at the men he hated.

In case any intelligence correspondence was captured by the enemy, Tallmadge, Washington, and Scott came up with aliases to use when writing about the men involved in this work. Tallmadge would be known as "John Bolton." The reckless Brewster stuck with his own name. Woodhull was given a name that referenced Charles Scott's initials, Washington's teenage employment in Culpeper County, and Tallmadge's younger brother Samuel.

Woodhull would be known as "Samuel Culper."

Local Connections

The running of the new intelligence service was not entirely smooth. Scott clashed with any subordinate who could threaten his position, and Tallmadge's combination of good work and contacts ensured he fitted this description.

More importantly for their mission, the two men favoured very different approaches to intelligence gathering. Scott was a traditionalist. He wanted to send scouts across enemy lines on short-term missions to collect specific information, as had happened with Hale. This was a tried and tested method that did not run the central risk of a spy ring - that if one person was caught and questioned, their revelations could lead to the capture of everybody else. Tallmadge, on the other hand, wanted to expand upon the methods Sackett had established, planting a network of long-term agents with cover stories. This could provide a better source of ongoing intelligence.

At first, Washington favoured the traditional scheme. But in mid-September, the British tightened up their perimeter guard procedures, leading to the capture of several of Scott's scouts. By the end of the month, Washington had become persuaded he should try Tallmadge's approach. As Tallmadge began building his network, often sidestepping Scott, the more senior man stepped aside. Making his excuses near the end of October, he resigned from intelligence work, leaving it to Tallmadge.

The new network Tallmadge built was based around Brewster and Woodhull. The three men came from the same community. Their families had known each other for generations. Brewster and Woodhull trusted Tallmadge and insisted on making him their only channel for information to Washington. Local connections and personal loyalty bound the spy ring together.

On his return to Long Island, Woodhull was at first viewed with suspicion by the Loyalist authorities. But not long after, the British offered pardons for revolutionary activity to any man willing to swear an oath of loyalty to the King. Woodhull swore the oath, painting a picture of himself as a believer in the Loyalist cause.

On the 29th of October, Woodhull sent his first written report. These early reports were copied out by Tallmadge and the originals destroyed, so not even Woodhull's handwriting could connect him to the information. Tallmadge later started sending original reports to headquarters, reducing their security and leaving an evidence trail for later historians to follow.

Woodhull's job had two parts - acting as a contact for Brewster and travelling into New York to gather information. The latter was the more awkward and dangerous part for him. He had to pass questioning at British checkpoints, buy permits to travel into the city, bear the costs of staying away from home, and neglect his duties of caring for his parents and the family farm. It reflected his passion for the Patriot cause that he bore these burdens.

Woodhull's early reports were of mixed quality. Information on troops was vague, unhelpful, and in at least one case inaccurate. But he provided information on the provisioning of the British and Loyalists, information which was vital to Washington in understanding the state of his enemies and how they might act.

The Circle Expands

Woodhull quickly began recruiting others to help him with his information gathering and so to spare him repeated trips into the city.

His first recruit was Amos Underhill, the husband of Woodhull's sister, Mary. A former mill owner, Underhill moved into New York after his property was destroyed by the British during Battle of New

York. He became a merchant and took in boarders to help pay the bills, including Woodhull during his trips into town. Supplies were short in a city cut off from the mainland and filled with soldiers and Loyalist refugees. Every penny counted for Underhill and his family.

On the 23rd of November, Woodhull provided a report that more than made up for his previous vagueness. He provided the names of commanders and units in the British occupation force, as well as their movements. In addition to this information, which Washington had requested, he provided something else - estimates of numbers. Washington had not asked for these, as estimates from previous agents had been unreliable. But Woodhull's were convincing and useful.

Though Woodhull was proving his value as an asset, he was also proving awkward to run. He insisted on only sending messages out through the trusted Brewster. But Brewster could not be provided with a permanent boat crew to carry messages across the Sound, as this would risk drawing attention to their activities. Getting messages out promptly was difficult.

One peculiarity of the agents of the Culper Ring, especially Woodhull, was their attitude toward their work. This sort of intelligence gathering was looked down upon in Europe and its American colonies. As a result, the agents did not like to think of themselves as spies. They went to great lengths to find other ways to refer to their work. They did not accept payment for their work, as this would have been an acknowledgment that they were spies, even though it would have been incredibly valuable to a man such as the struggling Woodhull. He kept careful notes of all the expenses he incurred while undertaking "this business" and his reports included details of these costs as well as insistence they be paid. Financially, he could not afford to be at a loss thanks to his intelligence gathering. But personally, he could not afford to acknowledge what he had become or to make it official through wages.

Reimbursing Woodhull was made difficult because he could not be paid in Congress's paper money, which was no use inside occupied New York. The British currency or bullion he wanted was more valuable than the inflation-ravaged Congressional cash, as well as harder to obtain. One of the tensions between Washington and Woodhull came from the general's insistence that the spy be economical in his expenses, a comment that offended Woodhull until Washington explained the currency problem. Finances would poison their working relationship throughout the war.

Despite the tensions and practical challenges, the spy ring was now firmly in place and providing valuable intelligence. Washington could be pleased with the network that history would know as the Culper Ring.

Communication Problems

Over the winter of 1778-9, military campaigning quietened down. This gave Tallmadge the time he needed to iron out the wrinkles in the Culper Ring.

The most critical challenge was to get the intelligence through more quickly. Though things weren't moving fast over winter, information still needed to be timely to have much value. The energetic Brewster could carry messages across the Sound quickly, but issues on land added delays.

The issues on the Connecticut side were easy to address, as they came within the control of the military. Arranging meetings between Tallmadge and Brewster delayed the reports reaching the Patriot chain of command, as did getting through checkpoints set up to stop enemy agents.

To deal with this, a regular chain of dragoon riders was stationed at Danbury, to receive messages from Brewster and carry them to the army camp. Though the riders had no idea who these messages were from, they must have recognised their importance thanks to both their orders and the special passes they were given, providing permission to pass swiftly through the American lines.

It was more challenging to deal with delays on the New York side. Woodhull was doing most of his spying out of Underhill's house in the city. This was 55 miles away from Brewster's pickup point, a quiet, wood-shrouded bay outside Setauket. Carrying messages there dragged Woodhull away from New York and took travel time.

To get around this, Tallmadge recruited two men to act as couriers. Jonas Hawkins and Austin Roe were again members of established Setauket families, men who Woodhull and Brewster knew and who had been open about their Patriot sympathies early in the war. Though not as deeply involved in spying as Woodhull and Brewster, they risked their lives carrying secret messages out of New York to be shipped across the Sound.

The result was a radical improvement in the timeliness and frequency of reports. By the end of January 1779, a report which would previously have taken at least two weeks to reach Washington was in his hands in only seven days.

Chapter Three: Teething Troubles

The Limits of Intelligence

In late February, Washington received letters simultaneously from Brewster and Woodhull. They showed the sort of intelligence the Culper Ring could gain just by observing what was happening inside occupied territory.

Brewster's brief report was mostly about naval matters. The British were repairing and building flat-bottomed craft. This told Washington they were preparing to make a sea-borne assault, something the British had become particularly adept at during the war. The most likely target was Connecticut, and so the general knew to prepare for such an attack.

The other important part of Brewster's report was that privateer ships were being prepared. These were government-sanctioned pirates, setting out to attack enemy merchant shipping, depriving opponents of supplies and helping to fund the war effort. Both sides used them, but the British were far more effective. The Patriots warned their merchant suppliers that more such vessels were coming.

The recruitment of Hawkins and Roe as couriers had freed up Woodhull from his journeys to meet Brewster, allowing him to spend more time observing the British. This was reflected in a long and detailed report that ran to seven pages. As well as confirming what Brewster had said about the preparation of flat-bottomed boats, Woodhull gave a detailed account of which British units were in the city, which commanders were overseeing them, and what their total numbers were. This showed troops were being gathered at the northern tip of Manhattan, providing an early warning of the next British move.

What that move would be was unclear to Washington and his commanders. The British were building a new flotilla of transports, while at the same time allowing William Tryon, the royal governor of New York, to launch overland raids against American military stockpiles. Tryon, a staunch Loyalist who advocated punitive attacks against civilian supporters of the Patriot cause, was finally being let off the leash. Did this mean the invasion fleet was for him? If so, a raid into Connecticut by Tryon and his men seemed like the logical result. But there was little way of being sure.

This reflected the limits of what the Culper Ring could achieve. They observed troop movements, ships, and supplies, even the presence of senior officers in the city. But they had no way of learning what those officers were discussing among themselves.

In fact, General Henry Clinton was planning on putting Tryon and his men onto those boats, not as his primary summer strategy but as a distraction. If his plan worked, it would draw Washington away from his current position and supply depots. Clinton would then march out of New York and, by threatening supply lines, force Washington to meet him on ground of the British commander's choosing.

The work of the Culper Ring told Washington none of this. All it allowed him to do was to prepare a response to Tryon's strike, the exact action Clinton wanted.

Washington urged Tallmadge to find a way to get the Culper reports to him more quickly. They needed insight into what Clinton was doing, cutting through the fog of uncertainty about his plans. And for it to be relevant, they needed that insight as promptly as possible.

To speed up the process of reporting, Washington looked to recruit another agent in New York, so that Woodhull could oversee and coordinate operations from Setauket. Given Washington's frustration at Woodhull's character, he may also have wanted an agent he could work with more easily.

This led to a significant misstep by Washington.

Lewis Pintard was a Patriot merchant living openly in occupied New York. General Howe had agreed to let Washington have him as a representative in the city, ensuring that prisoners held by the British were adequately cared for. As part of the agreement, Washington promised not to use Pintard to obtain intelligence.

But by May 1779, the general was becoming desperate enough that he was willing to break his word to get information. He contacted Pintard through an intermediary, sounding him out about the possibility of acting as a spy.

Pintard was insulted by the offer and flatly refused. Despite this, and despite his discretion, rumours spread in New York that he was an American agent sent to spy on the British. He was forced to give up his position helping prisoners and to leave New York.

Washington's eagerness to improve his intelligence was understandable, but it was leading to mistakes as it ran up against the limits of the Culper Ring.

Secret Writing

Though Washington was interested in the speed of the messages, Tallmadge was more concerned with secrecy. The agents putting themselves at risk were men he had known since he was young, whose lives were intertwined with his. The example of his friend Nathan Hale had shown how badly things could go for a spy if he was caught. Tallmadge did not want that to happen to one of his agents, especially given the warning of Scott and others that the capture of one member of a network could lead to the capture of them all.

The Culper letters did not use the agents' real names. But this only protected their identities from leaking out within the Patriot army and so reaching the ears of the enemy. If one of the agents was caught with a report, the deception of names would do them no good. It would be obvious from the content of the letter they were a spy. They would be dead as surely as Hale.

Some way was needed to conceal the messages.

The first solution was provided to Washington by John Jay, future president of Congress and coauthor of the Federalist Papers. Jay's brother, Sir James, was a professional doctor and amateur chemist living in London at the outbreak of the war. He had used his chemistry skills to develop a system of invisible ink consisting of two separate parts, what we would now call an agent and a reagent. The agent was used to write on plain paper, becoming invisible almost immediately afterward. It only became visible when the reagent was later applied to the sheet. By writing in this way, the message could be made to look like nothing more than blank paper.

Sir James' invisible ink had already played a part in the revolutionary conflict, as he used it to send a report from London of the British government's decision to bring the colonies into line by force. When he left London and returned to America, he brought with him the secret of his chemical formula. It was hard to produce, requiring the right equipment and difficult to obtain ingredients. But once John Jay got Washington's interest, the general helped Sir James to get the necessary chemicals from medical supplies. Soon, John Jay was providing Washington with invisible ink, carried to him under the label of medicine.

One of the great advantages of secret writing was it had been considered and discarded by most intelligencers then at work. The known methods of invisible writing involved organic substances such as lime juice and milk. These were revealed by heating the document, either with a candle or iron, which turned the writing brown. This method was widely known and could be easily tested for - anyone with a naked flame could make the writing visible. As a result, it was hardly safe from prying eyes.

Sir James' chemical ink, therefore, came as a revelation, one that much excited Washington. He provided Sir James with the resources he needed and set him to work on providing both agent and reagent.

The Culper Ring received their first consignment of the ink in April 1779. It was still hard to produce, and so it took many months before they had a substantial supply. Woodhull, ever cautious, hoarded his ink long after he could have used it more regularly, a habit that infuriated Washington.

Under Pressure

The strain of his work had begun to tell on Abraham Woodhull. He was already uncomfortable with his position as a spy. It was dangerous work that took him away from his family and his farm. He keenly felt the gap in education between him and his immediate superior, Tallmadge, a Yale graduate whose greater eloquence and learning showed in their correspondence and conversations. This sense of inferiority added to his doubts about acting as a spy.

In mid-April, Tallmadge joined Brewster on his boat and risked a journey into enemy territory to meet with Woodhull at Setauket. It turned out that a pair of British officers had taken up residence in the settlement, and so Tallmadge had to hide out in the woods, sleeping rough for five days. But this still let him fulfill his mission, as Woodhull brought him food and the two talked about their work. Tallmadge reassured Woodhull that Washington appreciated his efforts, whatever the differences in perspective that showed in their correspondence. The general and the spy shared common ground in wanting messages to get through faster. Fifty guineas brought by Tallmadge helped to cover Woodhull's expenses, relieving the extra stress that came with financial hardship.

But ultimately, Woodhull still wanted out of the spy game. He was not going to quit unilaterally, but he made clear that, if Washington and Tallmadge offered him the option, he would stop in a heartbeat.

Aside from offering Woodhull some reassurance, this meeting resulted in an abortive effort to create a quicker communication line for the Culper reports. Woodhull agreed in principle to recruiting a permanent agent in Staten Island, found by Washington and Tallmadge and approved by Woodhull, who would carry his letters out of New York.

In practice, this idea only went to highlight the different priorities of Woodhull and Washington. Woodhull, concerned with protecting himself, would not enter Staten Island, one of the most heavily guarded British strongholds and a place he would be hard-pressed to justify visiting. If Washington wanted him to approve an agent, that agent would have to meet him outside Staten Island. But without someone going to Staten Island, Washington had no way to even find such an agent. The scheme stalled, and the Ring went back to the status quo, though with less help from the courier Jonas Hawkins, who cut back on his activities, once again slowing the transmission of reports.

Busted

In his eagerness to conserve invisible ink for his agents, Washington kept writing his responses to them and orders to Tallmadge in ordinary ink. So it was that, when the British intercepted a letter from Washington to Tallmadge on the 13th of June 1779, they could read its contents without difficulty. The letter mentioned C_r - a reference to Woodhull's codename of Samuel Culper - and the use of a "liquid."

Based on this letter, the British decided to raid Tallmadge's camp, in hopes of getting more information. At five in the morning on the 2nd of July, Colonel Banastre Tarleton led a force of 200 men in this attack. They captured eight men and twelve horses before being driven off by the dragoons and local militia, inflicting ten casualties on the Americans along the way. Most critically, they captured Tallmadge's horse and with it his saddlebags, which held another of Washington's plain ink letters.

This letter mentioned a man named George Higday who lived in Manhattan. He had previously helped stranded American officers to escape to New Jersey, and Washington thought he might hold potential as an agent. Here, in writing any man could read, Washington encouraged Tallmadge to recruit him.

The British arrested Higday and interrogated him. The poor man had played no part in Washington's spy games, but now he faced the risk of hanging as a revolutionary agent. He seems to have persuaded the British that he was not a man worth their attention, as after signing a fictionalised account of his contacts with Washington he disappeared.

Higday's arrest deprived Tallmadge of an opportunity, however tenuous, to recruit an agent. More importantly, the captured letters told the British that the Americans had an intelligence operation up and running on Long Island and that Tallmadge ran it. Previously ignorant of the ring's existence, they were now on the lookout for the mysterious C_r.

Codes

Tarleton's raid and Higday's arrest alerted Tallmadge to the danger his people were put in anytime an undisguised letter was sent as part of their work. He wanted to make sure no such letters were ever sent again. Given the shortage of Jay's invisible ink, he had to use a different solution - codes.

There was no shortage of codes available to governments and intelligence specialists around the world. In Europe, courtly intelligencers - a breed who received none of the scorn reserved for men like Hale and Woodhull - worked with a wide range of different cyphers, while counter-espionage organisations laboured to decrypt them. In America, several men of learning took an interest in the craft.

But Tallmadge was not a professional secret agent, and he did not have access to cryptographic experts. He had no opportunity to train his agents in complex deciphering techniques or to regularly provide them with new code books. He would therefore have to work with something more limited.

Woodhull was already using numbers to refer to New York, Setauket, and his two couriers. Building on this, Tallmadge developed a more detailed substitution code. He picked 710 relevant words out of the dictionary, as well as 53 proper names, people and places likely to come up in correspondence. Each word was assigned a number to stand in for it. Letter substitution was used for digits and words not covered in the dictionary, with a double line underneath to make clear that they should be decoded differently. Squiggles marked changes of tense and plurals.

The idea for this may have come from the Marquis of Lafayette, a French courtier and friend of Washington. It was unsophisticated by European courtly standards but cutting edge by the measure of what was happening in America. It would be two more years before this relatively simple substitution was widely used in the war.

The Culper Ring soon adjusted to using Tallmadge's code. They were now the most professional spies on Washington's side, on the way to earning their legendary status.

Chapter Four: Rearrangement

The Shadow of Suspicion

In the summer of 1779, the ever-cautious Woodhull felt the danger mounting.

John Wolsley, a privateer sailing out of Connecticut, was seized by the British. Scrabbling around for any information that might preserve his own life and freedom, he passed on a rumour he hadheard in Connecticut that Woodhull was up to something.

This information was received by John Graves Simcoe, colonel of the Queen's Rangers. Colonel Simcoe went to Setauket to hunt out Woodhull, but missed him by a day, as he had gone back to New York to continue his spy work. Unable to question Abraham Woodhull, Simcoe instead harassed his innocent and ageing father. On his return, Woodhull learned he was in grave danger.

Fortunately, he had a friend who could help him out. Colonel Benjamin Floyd was a Loyalist militiaman. Far from the most reliable character in the region, his Loyalist leanings were strong enough for him to sign up for the militia, but not enough for him to choose an active part in the war over sitting it out in Setauket. His property was plundered by both sides. Governor Tryon carried off his food while raiding Patriots, then Patriot raiders robbed him of cash and furniture and took him prisoner. Following the latter incident in 1778, Woodhull secretly asked Washington to have Floyd released, a move which provided him with a valuable supporter the following year.

Floyd, ever vulnerable to personalities stronger than his own, believed Woodhull's protestations that he was innocent of spying. The colonel stepped in, assuring the British command that Woodhull was a Loyalist, and he was once again left in peace.

Woodhull felt confident he was still in danger of being caught. With the shadow of suspicion hanging over him, he decided he could not continue his work in New York, and so retreated to Setauket. As he did so, he promised Washington he would find a man to replace him in New York, an agent he could manage from out in the countryside.

The New Man

Woodhull already had a man in mind. Within days of informing Washington of his intention, he returned to New York for what he hoped would be the last time in the war. There he recruited Robert Townsend, known in correspondence as Samuel Culper, Junior, or in Tallmadge's code numbers as 723.

Woodhull had met Townsend as a fellow resident of Amos Underhill's boarding house in New York. Townsend came from Oyster Bay in Long Island. His father was a Quaker, though one who enjoyed the fine things in life more than most. His mother was an Episcopalian. His local community leaned heavily toward the Loyalist cause, though passively, accepting British rule rather than fighting for it. His father, on the other hand, had worked hard to try to pull Oyster Bay into the Patriot cause. Robert Townsend came from a deeply divided background, in which expressing his views was sure to draw disapproval from someone.

Steering clear of his father's political agitating, the younger Townsend joined a merchant house in New York, the sort of apprenticeship that shaped many other young New Yorkers, including Alexander Hamilton. From there, he went on to set up his own store in 1773.

Townsend's outward appearance of political neutrality briefly cracked during the British invasion of New York in 1776. He signed up for the Patriot cause and was appointed commissary to General Nathaniel Woodhull, the relative whose death turned the nervous Abraham Woodhull into a convinced Patriot. It was a natural role for Townsend, the experienced provisioner, but not one he got to make a mark in. Only days after Townsend's appointment, General Woodhull was cut off and captured by the British. The young commissary retreated home, while the Loyalists and British took control of the region.

The decision of the Townsends, along with a sizable minority of Quakers, to break with their church's pro- Loyalist pacifism was inspired by the writings of another son of a Quaker - Thomas Paine. Paine's *Common Sense*, one of the most influential political tracts of the period, was influenced by Quaker ideas and language. But like many contemporary Quakers, Paine emerged from his principles determined to engage with and transform society, rather than to retreat from the world and focus on his righteousness. It was an argument that struck a chord with the bookish, half-Quaker Robert Townsend, and that drew him, however briefly, into the war.

In the aftermath of the invasion, both Townsend and his father made peace with the British cause. They swore their loyalty to the crown and kept their heads down. Most other religious factions on the continent sided with the British against the Presbyterian-dominated Patriots, while the Quakers, with their strong tendency toward pacifism and their opposition at the time to fighting legitimate authority, maintained a Loyalist-oriented neutrality. Townsend's brief activities for the Patriots had probably gone unnoticed by most. To outward appearances, he looked like he had accepted British rule.

Townsend returned to his commercial activities. He made the most of the occupation, specialising in selling to British and Loyalist military men. He provided grog to sailors and ingredients for punch to officers. Some of his earnings were invested in buying a share in James Rivington's coffeehouse, a popular spot among officers. Despite some initial difficulties, he did well financially out of the occupation, winding up with a substantial disposable income.

While he thrived, he saw people around him having a far harder time. Long Island had become home to a large British army which treated it as much like an occupied enemy country as like a liberated friendly one. Queens County, where Townsend came from, was treated particularly badly, and he heard stories about many injustices. Food, livestock, and fuel were taken from the locals by soldiers. In the immediate aftermath of battle, this was indiscriminate looting, in which everybody was treated with equal disregard. Once things settled down, the British officially only confiscated property from Patriots, but it was common for Loyalists also to suffer. Horses and wagons were requisitioned for the army, with quartermasters skimming off the compensation the government offered for this property. The same thing happened when trees were chopped down for fuel.

The legal rights supposedly granted to all Englishmen were curtailed in a war zone where military rules applied. Given free reign to vent their worst tendencies, many British officers revealed themselves to be vicious, murderous thugs far from the idealised protectors Loyalists had expected to meet.

Among the worst was Colonel Simcoe, the commander of the Queen's Rangers and the man who had beaten Abraham Woodhull's father while in pursuit of the spy. In the winter of 1778-9, Simcoe settled in Oyster Bay with his regiment and other British troops. He ransacked the town for wood, using it to build a fort overlooking the town. Planks from churches became firewood. The Quaker meeting house, a centre for loyal pacifism, was turned into an arsenal watched over by armed guards. A curfew was introduced, enforced by armed patrols who whipped those who defied them.

The Townsend family experienced one of the most significant impositions. They owned Raynham Hall, the most exquisite house in Oyster Bay, and so naturally Simcoe billeted himself, his staff, and visiting friends there. Robert's sister was subjected to the romantic attentions of Simcoe.

Visiting Oyster Bay that winter, Robert saw firsthand the behaviour that would turn many Loyalists into Patriots over the course of the British occupation. Outraged at the treatment of his friends and family by Simcoe and his men, he was primed for the invitation that would come his way the following year - a call to once again act in the Patriot cause.

Learned and thoughtful, Townsend spent a lot of time reading and making notes on what he read, which ranged from the philosophy of Montesquieu to trade magazines and London journals. He was prone to depression, driven in part by his divided identity and the sense that he could not reveal his true self.

Slowly, carefully, Woodhull sounded out Townsend about his political leanings, revealing his position as a secret Patriot. In June 1779, he asked him if he would be willing to serve the American cause, and Townsend said that he would.

Townsend was a reserved and secretive sort, well suited to the cautious Woodhull, who now confided in him all the secrets of his spy work. Townsend was fearful of taking part in such dangerous activities but agreed under great persuasion from his friend. There were conditions attached to his recruitment that no-one else would know who he was, except for the courier who received his messages - at this point Austin Roe.

Work as a spy helped Townsend to deal with his divided identity. Deceiving others about his views was no longer an act of self-preservation - it was work toward a more noble cause. A worthy cause that would give him the chance to avenge the men who had treated his family and community so disgracefully. A cause that would let him act on the principles that Paine's *Common Sense* had seeded in his heart.

As Townsend's business put him in regular contact with the occupiers, he was well positioned to gather information about their activities. Now that information would have a channel to the Patriots.

A Complete Network

Tallmadge now had a complete chain of intelligence gathering and transmission. Townsend would gather information and record it using codes and invisible ink. Hawkins and Roe would carry it to Setauket and pass it to Woodhull in person or via a dead drop. Woodhull would add his and the couriers' information, then signal Brewster to pick up the reports. On the far side of the Sound, Tallmadge would receive the documents from Brewster, develop the invisible ink, add his information and analysis, and hand the complete packet to a dragoon. This courier would carry it to Washington.

A team of well-connected men was turning their skills and knowledge, together with the specialist tools of espionage, to Washington's cause.

Chapter Five: The Culper Ring at Work

Countering Clinton

Townsend quickly sets to work. Just over a week after Woodhull recruited him, he sent his first report down the chain to Washington.

This report was limited in its contents and awkward in its style. Townsend didn't yet have the Code Dictionary that the Culper men would soon use in encoding and decoding their reports, so he had to write in ordinary English. To avoid incriminating himself if the letter fell into British hands, he dissembled, creating what looked like a letter from one Loyalist to another, describing what he had seen happening in New York.

Despite the difficulties of communication, the letter contained a useful warning. Two British divisions were preparing an attack on Connecticut. Woodhull had heard rumours of similar activity, which he passed on. It was clear the British were up to something, but precisely what remained a mystery.

Days later, the British launched their attack. The pieces the Culper Ring had struggled to put together over the preceding six months started falling into place.

On the 4th of July, Governor Tryon led 2,600 men into the transports that Woodhull and Brewster had seen being prepared over the winter. The next day, they launched the first in a series of raids on the opposite shore, designed to draw out Washington. Over the course of a week, they attacked New Haven, East Haven, Fairfield, and Norwalk. This was Tryon's chance to carry out the sort of devastating raid he had long advocated. His men took what they wanted and burned the rest down. Ships, homes, barns, even schoolhouses, and churches went up in flames. Tryon and his men stole tens of thousands of dollars' worth of property before retreating across the waters to the safety of Long Island.

Elsewhere, Colonel Tarleton was part of the advance screen covering for Sir Henry Clinton's force, who would fall in behind Washington, aiming to bring the Patriots to battle in conditions that favoured the British. It was during this screening work that Tarleton tried to capture Tallmadge, leading to the critical capture of the second uncoded letter.

The Culper Ring warned Washington of the coming attack. But while their information set out in advance of the British and was delivered in only five days, it still arrived after the action had begun. It wasn't until the 7th of July that Washington read the report and sent an urgent message to Governor Jonathan Trumbull, warning him to prepare against attacks that had already occurred.

While the immediate warning of Tryon's attack arrived too late, the Culper Ring had already provided the information that kept Washington from falling for Clinton's trap and rushing to stop the diversion. The intelligence gathered since the winter told him that Clinton was preparing for a more prominent push. Even as Trumbull begged for help, Washington sat tight, unwilling to give the British an opening to seize control of the Hudson River, a vital transport link.

On the 11th of July, Washington received word that Clinton was advancing. He ordered General William Heath to provide a screen against the British army while most of his forces stayed put. Then, on the 15th of July, General "Mad Anthony" Wayne led a force of Patriot light infantry in a dramatic assault on the British-held fort at Stony Point. Caught by surprise by a midnight bayonet charge, their numbers already reduced to support Tryon's raiding, the Stony Point garrison was swiftly overwhelmed. More than 60 men were killed and 553 captured. The fort returned to American hands.

Not only had Clinton's strategy been thwarted through superior intelligence work, but he had lost a strategically and symbolically crucial strong point. To top it off, Tryon's raiding caused outrage, turning more people against the Loyalist cause. Clinton's ambiguous orders had left Tryon space to commit atrocities, but now Clinton blamed him and used this as his outlet to vent his frustrations, creating a rift between the two commanders.

Settling In

The addition of Townsend to the Culper Ring proved valuable in other ways. He soon provided details of a Loyalist, Christopher Duychenik, sent to spy on the Patriots. His mere presence initially improved Woodhull's mood, as the pressure of being Washington's sole source of information from inside New York was lifted. Now he could settle into managing Townsend. He took care to meet with him again and reiterate his instructions, to ensure the Ring's careful system of deception was maintained.

Managing another agent provided its challenges. Townsend's attitude to accommodating spying around the rest of his life was different from Woodhull. Townsend wasn't willing to give up his business to commit his time to espionage, as Woodhull had expected. And unlike Woodhull, he wanted to be rewarded for his work - not necessarily through money, but through a public office provided by the American government once it won the war. This mercenary attitude was very much at odds with Woodhull's strained, almost martyred approach to spying, something he did out of duty but with a sense of resentment.

Fortunately, Washington assured Townsend, via Woodhull, that he would be suitably rewarded for his service once the war was over. He also pointed out to Woodhull the advantages of Townsend continuing in business alongside his espionage work. It would provide him with a cover, with security, and with opportunities to gather information that might not otherwise be available. What Woodhull had initially seen as a hindrance to Townsend's work for the Ring was turned around into an advantage, a way of ensuring their work continued smoothly and efficiently.

Meanwhile, the strains of their work were telling on Jonas Hawkins, one of the two couriers who carried the Ring's letters out of New York. Signs of Hawkins' fragility had been increasingly apparent over the course of 1779. Like Woodhull, he was feeling the strain of living a double life and putting himself in danger, and he had made himself less available to carry messages. He had fallen so far from the heart of the Ring that, when Tallmadge created his code, he didn't even include a number specifically for Hawkins.

The growing danger of travelling in and out of New York finally became too much. Travellers were harassed by both the authorities and muggers on the roads. A lone man who deliberately kept away from others was particularly vulnerable to criminals and suspicious to the authorities. The capture of two Culper letters over the summer, confirming as it did that messages were being regularly transmitted in and out of the city, ensured British and Loyalist troops were on the lookout for anyone who might be a covert messenger. In August, Hawkins had a close call when troops closed in on him, and he had to destroy a letter to avoid being caught.

In September, Hawkins refused to come into the city to pick up a letter, instead insisting Townsend come out to Long Island to meet him. Townsend, who had not been working under pressure for as long as the rest, believed the courier's fears were imaginary. He refused to cooperate anymore with Hawkins, who slipped out of the Ring, probably to his great relief.

Friends and Allies

Woodhull was still making occasional trips into New York. For at least one of these journeys he recruited the help of Anna Strong, his neighbour and the wife of a distant relative who was then rotting in a British prison ship. By travelling with her, Woodhull could create the illusion of a married couple on the road. This was less likely to draw the attention of patrols, who were looking out for lone men acting furtively.

Strong, like Amos Underhill, played a supporting role in the Ring. Others also made occasional appearances in their work.

One of the most significant was Captain Nathan Woodhull, Abraham Woodhull's uncle. In his mid-fifties, Captain Woodhull leaned more toward the politics of the Whigs than that of the Tories, the core supporters of the British crown in the Americas. Despite this, he entered the war as a Loyalist rather than a Patriot, joining a militia on the British side. It is clear his loyalties shifted somewhere in the war, as did those of many moderates who experienced the unpleasantness of the British occupation. His first input to the Culper Ring, in September 1779, was to tell his nephew about a council of war and the embarkation of large numbers of troops onto transport ships. This could have been casual gossip, but two months later he provided information that confirmed he was deliberately feeding information to the Patriots - a detailed report on the positions of troops around Huntington.

Such insight from an officer inside the enemy army was incredibly valuable, and so Tallmadge and Washington set their sights on recruiting someone more senior, someone who would have better access to leading commanders and information on war plans, someone who, in their eyes, had already shown he was susceptible to being turned - Colonel Benjamin Floyd.

It is easy to see why Floyd caught the attention of the ambitious officers running the spy ring. He was the man who had covered for Woodhull when Colonel Simcoe was closing in on him, an act which demonstrated Floyd was either sympathetic to the Patriots or gullible and open to manipulation. The looting of his property by Loyalists was sure to have roused his resentment against the people he had sided with. Surely this was a Loyalist who could be turned?

To encourage Floyd's change of sides, Washington ordered the Patriot governor of New York, George Clinton, to stop revolutionary raiders attacking Floyd's property. Let him see that only the Loyalists were a problem and he would be open to siding against them.

With this done, Tallmadge approached Woodhull, asking him to recruit Floyd.

Woodhull refused. He and Floyd, distant relatives, had helped each other out. But Woodhull disliked Floyd, both personally and because of his Tory politics. Though he acknowledged the potential benefits of recruiting such a prominent man to the cause, he believed it also involved risk, as Floyd might turn on them. Given the weakness of character Floyd had previously shown, and which they were to some extent relying upon to recruit him, it is easy to see how Floyd might have given the game away or been turned against the Culper Ring by the British the moment he came under pressure. Better then to keep Floyd in place as an innocent dupe, able to cover for Woodhull in an emergency, sincere in his belief the man at the heart of the spy ring was a simple Loyalist farmer.

Improving Operations

The more time they spent spying, the craftier the Ring became in their methods.

Townsend came up with a way of making his messages harder for the enemy to hide. He would buy a set of new sheets of paper, write his message in invisible ink on one of the sheets, and insert it at a prearranged place in the papers. The batch of paper would draw less suspicion than a single blank sheet. Though a good plan in principle, it fell short when Tallmadge was not told in advance about which page the message would be on, and so had to use up precious reagent chemicals swabbing blank sheets until he found the right one. It was also a relatively expensive way of making messages, as good blank paper was purchased as an import from Britain.

Washington came up with a better solution. He suggested Townsend write his messages on the blank pages of pamphlets and books or between the lines of letters apparently written to acquaintances. These documents would provide a better cover for the blank space concealing the invisible writing. They would also be cheaper, as there were plenty of out of date almanacs and old pamphlets available in New York. Townsend happily adopted this solution, and the Ring continued sending messages, now in greater security.

As the Ring's activities became more regular, Washington sought to formalise them, increasing the professionalism of his spy network. In October 1779, he and Tallmadge wrote up a document giving instructions on how Woodhull and Townsend should carry out their work and what their employers expected from each man.

The document is interesting for the faith and ambition Washington clearly placed in his operatives, and for the way it reflects his priorities at the time. He wanted Townsend to find out:

- How many soldiers were in the city, from which corps, and where they were stationed.
- About the city's defences, including how many redoubts there were, how many cannons each contained, and whether there were stake-lined pits in front of the defences.
- How well the British army was provisioned.
- What the morale and health of the soldiers was like.

This was a lot of information for one man to acquire, including details that could only be got by close association with soldiers and inspection of military works, something he apparently thought Townsend could do without drawing unwanted attention.

Washington's focus on New York's defences stemmed from his ambition to make a move against the city. A French fleet under the Comte d'Estaing was said to be approaching the region. Washington hoped to persuade d'Estaing to support him in an assault on New York, the most powerful and important British centre of the war. If they could catch the British by surprise, then the Americans and French might be able to overwhelm their defences and take the city.

But any chance of such a surprise was lost. In early October, Townsend reported that General Clinton's scouts had spotted the approaching French fleet and the British were frantically preparing to defend the city against them. Hulks were placed ready to be sunk and so block the channel. Fire ships were prepared to attack the enemy ships. Garrisons were increased on approaches to the city, including in western Long Island, blocking any advance Washington might make out of Connecticut.

Disappointing as this news was for Washington, it confirmed the value of the Culper Ring, who had given him enough information to decide against a potentially disastrous attack.

That fall, General Clinton was also making plans to go on campaign, plans which he, like Washington, would have to abandon. The preparations led to an increase in troop activities and foraging in New York, which once again set Woodhull's nerves on edge. On the 10th of November, he was questioned by a party of more than 200 British foragers on his way to a meeting with Townsend, a meeting which Townsend missed. The incident inevitably played on the mind of the ever-twitchy Woodhull, who again made noises about leaving spying.

Then came another of the successes that made all the risk worthwhile. Townsend heard about a plan to hit the Americans where they were most vulnerable - in their economy.

The Patriots had struggled from the start to fund their war. The printing of paper dollars had given them a currency to work with, but it was one that suffered from rampant inflation, and which people were therefore wary of accepting. By the middle of 1779, it took 30 Continental dollars to buy a single silver dollar, and the Continental was trading at 200 dollars to the guinea in New York. This was why paying Woodhull in other currencies had placed an extra burden on Washington.

One of the reasons the currency suffered so badly was the British made deliberate efforts to undermine it. They had previously printed fake American currency, then spread exaggerated rumours of fakes to undermine what faith in the money remained. The fakes were printed on thicker paper than the originals, and so could be identified by a discerning eye, but that did not stop them drastically undermining the colonial economy.

The news that Townsend heard in the fall of 1779 was particularly disturbing. The British had acquired a batch of paper like Congress used to make its currency. They could print perfect copies which would flood the market without hope of being identified, completely wrecking the Patriots' economy.

This intelligence helped Congress to make a critical decision. They retired the current currency, recalling all the bills. If the British could forge their money, thenthey would stop using it. It was a difficult decision, one which added to their financial woes but saved them from worse problems down the line.

A Brush with Disaster

Washington was still eager to receive the Culper intelligence more quickly, and he was willing to put pressure on his agents to get it. He wanted a more direct route of communications, across the north river or through Staten Island, cutting through the circuitous system they had developed to avoid capture.

Woodhull was meant to discuss this with Townsend during a meeting at Christmas 1779 but forgot. Washington, who had long clashed with Woodhull, became increasingly annoyed and determined to cut him out of the Ring. Through Tallmadge, he encouraged Townsend to find hisown way of getting messages out of the city, using a more direct route. He offered some contacts, but Townsend was too cautious to trust anyone he had not found for himself. And so he settled on his teenage cousin, James Townsend.

James was sent across the Hudson in March 1780, carrying a message written in invisible ink between the lines of a love poem. The part of New Jersey he was going into, though controlled by the Patriots, was full of Loyalist sympathisers. He therefore used a cover story that he was himself a Loyalist, off to covertly recruit men for the British army.

Unfortunately, he wound up drinking in the house of Deausenberrys, a family of Patriots. They played the part of Loyalists to catch out this apparent British agent. Drunk and showing off to two young women, James gave his story about recruiting for the British. The family took him prisoner and dragged him to the local Patriot leaders, who found the pages of poetry.

When Washington found out what had happened, he had to go to great lengths to ensure James' release. The general was furious. If James had been this indiscrete around real Loyalists, he could have been giving away the secrets of his mission to the enemy, blowing the Culper operation. Washington had to expend time and effort getting a drunken, reckless teenager out of trouble. And to cap it all off, the letter had been so clumsily created that, when Washington applied the reagent to reveal the message, it became illegible.

Townsend was angry, embarrassed, and afraid that news of the business would get out, leading to his capture and execution by the British. Woodhull, briefed on the affair by Tallmadge, discovered Townsend had gone behind his back in trying to communicate directly with Washington, and had endangered them all by his unsuitable choice of courier. He went to talk with him in New York, at which point Townsend resigned as a spy. It was only after two more visits from Woodhull and intervention by Tallmadge that he was persuaded to keep gathering intelligence, though he insisted he would not write reports, only verbally pass on to Woodhull what he had seen.

Washington's patience with his awkward agents finally ran out. He decided thatthe information they gave was neither useful nor prompt enough to be worth the effort. Woodhull's regular requests for payment of expenses aggravated him. He shut down the operation, without acknowledging their achievements or paying Woodhull the money he was owed.

Rescuing Rochambeau

Once his anger had passed, Washington realised his mistake. The agents in New York could still be valuable. In July 1780, only two months after shutting down the Culper Ring, he sent Tallmadge to find out if it could be revived. Little did he realise how much he needed their help.

The reason for making contact was the approach of a French fleet, led by the Comte de Rochambeau. As with d'Estaing's earlier approach, Washington was hopeful he could persuade Rochambeau to help him seize New York. Tallmadge's mission was therefore twofold - to see if the members of the Culper Ring were willing to be re-engaged and to find out if they had heard anything about the coming of the French.

Tallmadge got lucky on his journey. Arriving at Fairfield on the 15th of July, he found Brewster in the harbour and was able to cross with him to Setauket that night. There, he found Woodhull lying in bed sick but Austin Roe available to ride to New York and talk to Townsend. Tallmadge, meanwhile, returned to Patriot territory.

Roe soon came back from New York with a report written in invisible ink, hidden on a fake order for merchandise allegedly written by Colonel Floyd, Woodhull's unwitting Loyalist beard. Townsend had news so important he was not just willing to rejoin the Ring but willing to put his information in writing, despite his earlier decision not to.

The British Admiral Graves had assembled nine ships of the line. Eight thousand British troops had embarked onto transports. This flotilla was heading for Rhode Island, to attack the newly arrived French.

The British effort was overseen by General Clinton, whose own spies had informed him the French were coming. He intended to attack them once they landed, while they were tired and unprepared. He would hammer them both on land and at sea, forcing a retreat. The Americans would lose this support, a significant military blow. Politically, it would make the French more reticent about involvement in the war, helping to isolate the rebels.

Brewster arrived in Connecticut with the report on the 21st. Unable to find Tallmadge, he sent a dragoon to headquarters. In Washington's absence, the message was received and deciphered by Alexander Hamilton, one of the general's closest aides. Realising the urgency of the situation, Hamilton sent riders to inform Rochambeau and the Marquis de Lafayette, who was heading to join the new French force.

Forewarned, the French and Americans were able to prepare for the British attack. Clinton, hearing about their military movements from his agents, gave up on the operation.

Rochambeau's force had been saved by the Culper Ring.

Back in Business

In the aftermath of the Rochambeau affair, the Culper Ring was reformed. Woodhull was willing to return to work for Washington, especially after the general paid him the money he was owed. He persuaded Townsend to continue their work, supported by a fresh promise from Washington of a government job after the war. Both men set to trying to find a faster way to send the messages to Washington and believed this might be possible via Cow Neck on Oyster Bay, allowing emergency messages to be received in 12 hours instead of several days. And both agreed they wanted to get rid of the courier Roe, who they found increasingly unreliable. Washington, acutely aware than Roe's rides to and from New York also accrued significant expenses, inclined to agree with this, but Tallmadge talked him out of cutting Roe loose just yet. The expenses were reasonable and the courier had done good work. There was no need to make a change until a better option was secured.

Chapter Six: The View from the Other Side

Clinton's Intelligence Services

While all of this was going on, the British had their own agents in play. They didn't have anything as sophisticated as the Culper Ring, and for a while, General Clinton did not have a head of intelligence, a man equivalent to Tallmadge who could have saved him from the day-to-day work and kept things running smoothly. None of the commanders appreciated the importance of timeliness and multiple sources in the way that Washington did. Their efforts were far more focused on military scouts, who were still important to the Americans, but whose limitations Washington had come to appreciate.

Part of the problem was the British were bogged down in a European view of intelligence. High-level espionage in Europe consisted of intercepting and decoding letters between diplomats and courtiers, a technique of little relevance in a continent without courts or a regular post service. Military manoeuvres in Europe took place within more confined spaces and well-known routes than in America, so scouting was more limited in its aims and potential than in the New World. While not consciously fighting a European war, Clinton was weighed down by the habits of one. And while both he and Washington had to develop a new way of working mainly from scratch, the American proved more adept at adjusting.

But the British did manage to establish agents in American territory, agents who had helped them during the Rochambeau plot. Two Loyalist officers ran private intelligence networks based out of New York - General Cortland Skinner and Colonel Beverley Robinson. Scouts, prisoners, deserters, and refugees provided them with a messy mix of information which they compiled into reports and sent to Clinton. Jumbles, contradictory, and seldom timely, these reports were of limited use.

But the most valuable agent, and the one who would become most notorious in the annals of history was General Benedict Arnold.

Major André

Major John André was the son of a Swiss father and a French mother. After growing up in Geneva, he moved to London to work for his father's mercantile company. After inheriting his father's wealth at 19, he bought a lieutenant's commission in the British infantry and went to fight in North America in 1775.

Captured by the Americans during a siege, André was exchanged after the Battle of New York. He joined General Howe's headquarters staff as a translator for the Hessians, German soldiers who made up a significant and colourful minority of British troops. After Howe's departure, he became part of Clinton's staff and one of his closest confidants.

In May 1779, Clinton was overwhelmed with work. He made André his intelligence specialist, delegating oversight of this part of the war effort to his trusted friend and aide. André began by sifting out intelligence reports from the rest of the general's correspondence and collecting them in chronological order. It might seem like a basic step, but it drew important information out from a mass of day-to-day business, making it accessible in one place. Abandoned due to disinterest in August, this system was picked up again in July 1780.

In the meantime, André had picked up a far more valuable source of information than any that had come before.

Benedict Arnold

Benedict Arnold had started out as a dedicated and courageous warrior in the Patriot cause. He fought bravely at the Battle of Ticonderoga and stopped General Burgoyne escaping the Americans at the Battle of Bemis Heights. But he did not feel he was suitably appreciated or rewarded for his efforts. Overlooked for promotion, he began to wallow in resentment against his peers and superiors.

Placed in charge of Philadelphia while he recovered from a leg wound, Arnold became engaged to Peggy Shippen, the daughter of a local loyalist. He was already drifting toward Tory politics, uncomfortable at his nation's alliance with France, the long-standing enemy of Britain and her colonies, and the engagement helped to solidify his position. His enemies sought to have him court-martialed for small misdemeanours, and though Washington saved him from any serious consequences, he still rebuked Arnold for his failings.

To sooth Arnold's damaged pride, Washington put him in charge of West Point, a position he took up in August 1780. But by then it was already too late - Arnold's heart had turned against the rebel cause.

In May 1779, Arnold met with Joseph Stansbury, a Philadelphia merchant. He asked Stansbury to act as his emissary, going to the British in New York and offering them Arnold's services as an agent. In New York, Stansbury's contacts in the Loyalist community introduced him to André, the newly made head of Clinton's intelligence services. André brought word of this to the general, who gave him permission to pursue the matter with Arnold.

So began an extended covert correspondence between André and Arnold. Like the Culper ring, they went through several iterations of encryption as they looked for a secure way to transmit dangerous messages. People and places were given dramatic code names taken from the Bible. Numerical codes were created through references to the placement of words in specific books - first a set of legal commentaries, then a dictionary. Arnold provided valuable information on the strength and location of Patriot forces as well as their supply depots. At the same time, he began negotiating the rewards for his betrayal of the American cause. He had felt under-appreciated and under-rewarded by his current masters. He was determined thathis new ones should not treat him the same way.

The first few months were a period of careful negotiation and testing for both sides. André was trying to work out whether Arnold was what he appeared to be and how much could be gained from his senior position, not just in information, but in potential disruption and even seizure of Patriot positions. Arnold was trying to work out how much he could get out of the British, his motives being far more mercenary than those of the Culper agents.

August 1780 was a turning point. Not only did Arnold take control of the garrison at West Point, a highly valuable position, but he and André agreed on the terms of his defection. If, as part of his defection, he managed to hand over West Point and its garrison to the British then he would be rewarded with £20,000. If that failed, but he still managed to defect, then he would receive £10,000. Either was a considerable sum - Washington had almost given up on the Culper Ring for sums below £100 - but worth it for the British given what was at stake.

Things Fall Apart

In September, André snuck into Patriot territory to meet with Arnold and seal the deal. Travelling up the Hudson River with one of his local agents, Beverley Robinson, André was at first chased off by a British patrol boat. On the 21st of September, André met with Joshua Smith, an intermediary for General Arnold, and through him was finally brought to Arnold.

They talked through most of the night, Arnold providing information about West Point and British forces. With daylight approaching, André decided to stay at Smith's house.

The next day, the ship that had brought André up the Hudson was shelled by American artillery, forcing it to retreat downriver. André was forced to set out overland, disguised as a civilian, carrying with him maps and sketches of local defences as well as a travel pass provided by Arnold.

On the 23rd, André was ambushed by three Patriots. Interested as much in mugging him as in furthering the political cause, they were negotiating how much he would have to pay them to secure his release when, in removing his expensive boots, they found the incriminating documents he was carrying. Deciding they might as well hand him in, they took him to Colonel Jameson, the commander at North Castle, who let them keep André's belongings in return for surrendering the prisoner.

Colonel Jameson was put in an awkward position. Here was a man, travelling under the name of James Anderson, trying to leave American territory with sensitive documents and a pass provided by General Arnold. Only days earlier, he had received instructions from Arnold to let a James Anderson travel into their territory from New York, and now he was going the other way, with suspicious papers and with Arnold's permission. Jameson was wary of what Arnold, his commanding officer, was up to, but aware he risked getting in trouble for insubordination if he went behind Arnold's back. Hedging his bets, he sent the papers directly to Washington and sent André, along with a report of the events, to Arnold.

Late that evening, Tallmadge arrived at Jameson's headquarters and heard the story. He had also received a letter from Arnold asking him to give James Anderson safe passage. Now a seasoned veteran in the art of covert operations, he jumped to the right conclusion. Unable to persuade Jameson to help him arrest Arnold, he managed to have André fetched back, though Jameson still insisted on sending the letter explaining the situation to Arnold.

In the light of the next day, André's captors noticed the powder in his hair as well as his military way of carrying himself. It was increasingly evident this was no mere civilian.

On learning thathis letters had been sent to Washington, André gave up. He wrote a letter to Washington giving his actual name and admitting he was a British officer.

Meanwhile, Arnold had been awaiting Washington's arrival to inspect West Point. He had hoped to kidnap the supreme commander of the American forces and take him with him to the British, a spectacular coup. But while he was waiting, the letter from Jameson arrived. Realising the game was up, Arnold fled to the British.

Fallout

The Americans rushed, too late, to arrest Arnold. They reinforced the defences at West Point in case of an impending British attack. They had been saved from a potentially massive disaster and were not going to take any risks with what they now knew.

Tallmadge rode with André to Tappan, well away from any prospect of a British rescue mission. The two men got on well. Tallmadge was sad to realise, and to reveal, that André's fate would likely be the same as that of Tallmadge's old friend Hale - execution for espionage.

The situation was more complex than it had been for Hale. André was adjutant general of the British army, and Clinton wrote to intercede on his behalf. Washington was willing to trade him for Arnold, but Clinton, though upset at losing his friend, could not make that trade if he ever wanted to see another defection. On Washington's side, the American public had to be appeased with the blood of one of the major players in the drama.

Tallmadge continued to provide his opposite number with support throughout the process and was the one who confirmed to him that he would hang as a spy rather than, as André had asked, being shot as an officer. André faced the gallows as Hale had done, with courage and dignity, his final words "bear me witness that I meet my fate like a brave man."

The British had lost their head of intelligence in a botched operation. But Arnold's defection was still a significant military coup for them, and one that became an eye-opener in their intelligence work.

Arnold brought with him a letter from Tallmadge, sent not long before the major discovered Arnold's betrayal. While not admitting the existence of a spy ring, it referred to information coming out of New York, information which Tallmadge had gained through the Culper Ring. The British started putting the pieces together. Tallmadge was based in southern Connecticut, territory full of smugglers running in and out of Long Island. The previous year, Colonel Simcoe had heard there was a spy in Setauket. Now information was being fed to the enemy out of New York. These elements wereclearly connected.

All the British had to do was capture one link in the chain - the smuggler, the New Yorker, the Setauket man, even Tallmadge himself - and they could dig out the agents in their midst.

Chapter Seven: After Arnold

Going Quiet

Before defecting, Arnold had done his best to find out about American spies on the British side. That so many survived his betrayal is a tribute to the discretion of men like Tallmadge, who gave their agents code names and went to great lengths not to discuss them unless absolutely necessary. Still, Arnold was determined to play his part in bringing down American spies, and with Clinton's permission, he began rounding up suspects in New York. Valuable agents were endangered, and the Culper Ring went quiet while they waited for the trouble to blow over.

When they contacted Tallmadge again, it was on cautious terms. Woodhull was willing to return to work, but Townsend was not, for now at least, and he ended efforts to find a shorter message route, preferring to trust to tried and tested men. As Washington kept pushing him to use a shorter route, Townsend became increasingly uncomfortable.

The breaking point for Townsend came when Arnold, in his attempts to round up American spies, unwittingly arrested a member of the extended Culper network.

Hercules Mulligan had been working as a spy since before the Ring was founded. A friend of Alexander Hamilton's, he shared Hamilton and Townsend's merchant background. He was recruited by Hamilton to provide information from inside New York. Well-connected in the city, he used his social and business contacts, as well as first-hand observations, to gather reports on British activities, just as Townsend did. Using his slave Cato as a courier, he transmitted these reports to Hamilton and Washington on the mainland. He also fed into the reports of Townsend, who he knew personally thanks to moving in the same social and business circles.

Mulligan's arrest was not triggered by any knowledge on the British part about his spy activities. It was known that he had leaned toward the Patriots politically at the start of the war, and so he became just one more target as Arnold went fishing for spies. Without any evidence against him, he was soon released.

This arrest and release had two effects on the Culper Ring. In the long term, it made it too dangerous for Cato to make his voyages across the water to deliver reports to the Americans, and so Mulligan instead channelled his information through Townsend. In the short term, it led Townsend to stop making reports for a while. He was too afraid Arnold was watching them and that, unless he was very careful, he might be arrested next.

Hunting the Traitor

For Washington, one of the most galling things about Arnold's betrayal was that the general had gotten away with it. And so, on the 14th of October, he gave Major Henry Lee the task of recruiting men to kidnap Arnold. He was determined Arnold should be brought back alive. It wasn't just a matter of vengeance - he wanted to make a public example of him.

Lee found two men - Sergeant John Champe and an anonymous contact in Newark.

Champe, who would play the leading part in the operation, was equipped with a small amount of money and the names of two contacts in New York. To get into the city, he was ordered by Lee to fake a desertion and defection to the enemy. Nobody could know the truth about what he was doing, not even his comrades in Lee's unit.

The mission almost ended in disaster on the very first night. Spotted by a patrol as he rode out on his fake desertion, Champe galloped away. The patrol reported to Lee, who pretended ignorance and did his best to delay. But his men were effective and quickly recognised that one of their own was missing. Lee had to send out a party to pursue Champe. Even the least effective of Lee's officers was good at his job. They tracked Champe down, and a chase ensued. He reached the Hudson River with his pursuers only a few hundred yards behind him and was rescued by a British boat, whose crew fended off the American troops with gunfire.

Following this dramatic escape, Champe was brought to General Clinton in New York. They talked for an hour, particularly about American morale and the likelihood of more defectors. Clinton recommended that Champe join a regiment of defectors and Tories being raised by Arnold.

It was a perfect opportunity. Champe quickly impressed Arnold, who made him a recruiting sergeant. He observed Arnold's routine and came up with a scheme to seize the general as he went on a regular midnight stroll around his garden. Through his New York contacts, Champe reached out to the volunteer in Newark, who contacted Lee and arranged for him and a group of dragoons to be ready with a boat at a discrete wharf on a set night, prepared to accept the captive.

But on the very day of the plan, Arnold was moved to new quarters as Clinton prepared to send him and his new unit into action. The plan fell apart. Champe was shipped out to fight for the British, along with the rest of Arnold's American Legion. Lee and his men waited on the river all night to no avail.

Months later, a bedraggled Champe arrived in Lee's camp, having deserted the British. Lee told the regiment the truth about his mission. Champe was rewarded and discharged from the army. Arnold remained none the wiser about the danger he had been in.

Long Island Raiders

While Townsend was unwilling to send reports out of New York, Tallmadge used the rest of the Culper Ring to other ends. By gathering information on activities on Long Island, he planned attacks against British troops and Loyalist privateers based there. Dealing with the privateers would be particularly useful, as they were one of the causes of delays in carrying reports across the Sound. As well as disrupting enemy military activities, this could speed up the Culper Ring's reports.

Throughout the war, a low-intensity conflict had been carried out in the Sound. Privateer crews from both sides had launched raids and kidnappings, smuggled supplies, and attacked each other. Named after the light, manoeuvrable vessels most of them sailed in, it was known as the Whaleboat War. Brewster had long played a part in the war, while on the opposite side, Colonel Simcoe cooperated with the Loyalist raiders.

The activities of both sides became a menace to the innocent inhabitants of Long Island. The privateers, given authority to raid those supporting the enemy military, went from taking the broadest interpretation of their orders to outright attacking civilians, as patriotic spirit gave way to naked profiteering. Long Islanders lived in terror of their raids, which along with British efforts to track down Patriot perpetrators disrupted the work of the Culper Ring. Even Brewster, who had himself been a whaleboat privateer, complained of the pain and damage inflicted by the raiders.

Washington leaned on Patriot governors to cancel the privateering licences on the Patriot side, but this had limited effect and did nothing to tackle the Loyalist raiders. Brewster, made his own ad hoc effort, attacking enemy privateers and taking some of them captive. But he and his crew could have only a limited effect on a much larger problem.

It was Tallmadge who finally took effective action. Thanks to his agents, he knew that Tory privateers lived in a camp outside Fort Franklin, under the protection of the fort's garrison. In September 1779, he and 130 of his dragoons left their horses behind and took passage in a flotilla of whaleboats led by Brewster. Under cover of darkness, they surprised the privateer camp, destroyed the boats and huts, took several prisoners, and escaped without loss.

The following August, Tallmadge, Brewster, and Woodhull plotted a raid against Fort Franklin, inspired in part by a spy planted there by General Parsons. Woodhull provided a sketch of the fort to prepare the troops with. But Tallmadge smelled a rat and called off the attack. He learned later that, as he had suspected, Parsons' spy was a double agent who had been leading them into a trap.

Woodhull repeatedly fed Tallmadge information about British and Loyalist troops in the area, encouraging the major to attack them. In November 1780, he provided the information that led to something more ambitious.

The British were accumulating hundreds of tons of supplies, mainly hay, at Coram, eight miles from Setauket. Eight miles further on, they were building a fortification on the south shore of Long Island, named Fort St. George. Tallmadge saw an opportunity to deprive the British of supplies and prevent them creating another coastal safe haven for privateers. At his request, Washington provided permission and 100 dragoons for him to launch another raid.

Once again accompanied by Brewster, Tallmadge and his dragoons crossed the Sound in whaleboats, then lay in hiding, waiting for the weather to improve. At dawn on the 23rd of November, they stormed Fort St. George, destroyed its stores and defensive works, and took 50 prisoners. A dozen men rode captured horses to Coram, where they chased off the guards and set fire to the enormous stock of hay. By mid-afternoon, they were back at their boats, and by one in the morning they were all safely back on the Connecticut shore. One of the raiders was severely wounded, but none were killed. The mission was considered such a success that Tallmadge received the thanks not only of Washington but also Congress.

Chapter Eight: Dying Days

Heron

Following André's death, Major Oliver De Lancey took charge of British counterintelligence work. He and his aides ran a more professional and impersonal operation than their predecessors and opposite numbers, with standardised code books and all their agents reporting to them as a group rather than being managed by a single individual. But no amount of procedures could balance a lack of proper experience, and De Lancey was about to be taken in by the lies of William Heron

Heron knew and was well respected by General Samuel Holden Parsons, a Patriot commander. Following Arnold's defection, Heron realised the British would pay handsomely for information about potential defectors high in the American ranks. So he went to De Lancey, shared information gleaned from General Parsons, and suggested the general might be persuaded to defect. De Lancey began employing him as an agent.

Back in Connecticut, Heron realised he could play both sides against each other. He gave Parsons information about the defences of New York, becoming his agent.

Heron moved back and forth between the two sides, giving each just enough information, some true and some invented, to keep them paying him. This also allowed him to carry out illegal and profitable trade across the lines, as both sides were letting him through.

Despite the vagueness of much of Heron's information, he convinced De Lancey that Parsons was ripe for defection. In return for his fictional accounts of Parsons' plans for defection, De Lancey gave Heron hundreds of pounds for Parsons, which Heron promptly pocketed.

Heron kept his scheme up until March 1782. By then, realism overcame De Lancey's optimism, and he realised Parsons was not going to defect. He lost interest in Heron, who was happy to move on, having made a substantial profit.

Crucially, one of the pieces of information Heron gave to De Lancey during their relationship concerned the Culper Ring. He told De Lancey that Brewster was carrying messages between Washington and his agents in Long Island, taking them through Setauket, and that Brewster was sheltered by "a certain woman" (unknown to Heron, this was Anna Strong). Now the British knew the identity of one of the links in the Culper chain and that he worked through Setauket. Was the trap finally going to close?

Culper Closes Shop

In January 1781, Woodhull met with Townsend in New York. He returned with good news - with the initial storm stirred by Arnold having died down, Townsend was willing to return to spying. The Ring seemed to be back in business.

Tallmadge's pleasure at this turn of events was deflated within months. No sooner had the Ring got back into action than it hit problems around the two themes that had disrupted its work in the past - money and security.

Financially, Washington had only himself to blame if his agents became discontented. Woodhull kept rigorous track of the Ring's expenses, asking for no more than what their work cost them, but this was not forthcoming. Payments had dried up again, and he was owed over a hundred pounds, a large sum to an ordinary colonial farmer. Townsend too had not been reimbursed for costs incurred in his work.

Woodhull recognised that it might be difficult for Washington to find the money immediately, given the costs of the war. He was willing to accept the situation for now if he was promised that the debts would be repaid with interest after the war. But he was not going to let the matter lie, and Washington had already shown he resented these requests for cash.

The other problem stemmed from getting reports out of New York. Austin Roe was increasingly reluctant to act as a courier. Neither Townsend nor Woodhull was willing to regularly make the journey. There had always been a risk inherent in those missions and now the danger had increased. The British had set up more checkpoints and recruited informers to report on suspicious activity, as they closed in on the agents they knew were working with Brewster and Tallmadge through Setauket. Anyone making repeated journeys through the checkpoints would become conspicuous, making capture likely.

Washington was persuaded to offer the Culper men suitable rewards, but in return, he wanted more regular reports. He got the opposite. Too afraid of capture, Townsend would no longer provide written reports. Woodhull, after some pointed questioning from the British, was unwilling to return to New York anytime soon.

From the summer of 1781, the Culper Ring ceased to exist as an ongoing enterprise. There were occasional letters from Woodhull and even rarer verbal reports from Townsend, but Tallmadge and Washington had to rely on temporary agents, some of them recruited from among Brewster's roguish crew.

A year later, with peace negotiations underway, Washington revived the Culper Ring to keep an eye on British activities in New York, in case they should make a last-minute attempt to keep control of the city. With the war approaching its end, things looked far less dangerous for the spies, and they took up their work again. But the reports were less informative and their recipients less attentive.

On the 21st of February 1783, Woodhull sent his last Culper report. The Ring's activities were over.

Conclusion: The Fates of the Culper Men

Brewster continued in Patriot employ throughout the war, often working alongside Tallmadge. He used his privateering activities to pursue vendettas against men he had clashed with on the opposite side, was wounded pursuing them during one of Tallmadge's raids, and for his successes received a pension and the praise of Washington. He married shortly after the war and had eight children. After working as a blacksmith, coastguard, and farmer, he died in 1827 at the age of 80.

The two couriers, Hawkins and Roe, both ran taverns after the war and were part of the same militia company. Roe died in 1830 at the age of 81. Hawkins disappeared from the historical record.

Townsend never received the public office Washington had promised him. He continued in business, supporting an illegitimate boy who may have been his son or may have been his nephew. After falling out with his brother and business partner Solomon, he retired to Oyster Bay, where he died in 1838 at the age of 84.

Shortly after the signing of the Treaty of Paris in September 1783, Tallmadge rode safely into British-occupied New York, the center of so many of his schemes. The British were withdrawing, so he went to ensure that his agents were safe during the chaos and recriminations that followed the occupation. He visited his family and friends in Setauket, celebrating the end of the war alongside many of the people who had been his agents. Like Brewster, he was married soon after the war, to Mary Floyd, a relative of Colonel Benjamin Floyd. He became wealthy from investments, was elected to Congress as a Federalist, and lived to the age of 81, dying in 1835. He left his spying activities out of records of his life and only spoke publicly about the work once, when André's capture came up in Congress. Losing his temper at praise for one of the men who caught the British spy, he railed against the selfish men who had tried to profit from the war, often at their country's expense, and who had only caught André while trying to rob him.

Abraham Woodhull, the nervous heart of the Culper Ring, was married twice - once in 1781, while he was still spying, and again in 1824, nearly 20 years after his first wife's death. He had three children by his first marriage, two of whom married Brewster boys. He died at the age of 75 in 1826, never having spoken about what he did during the war.

The Culper Ring survived through secrecy, and that habit clung to them through their long lives. It is only fitting that, generations later, the secrets of their work remain obscured - their courage remembered, but many of the details lost to time.

Check out another book by Captivating History

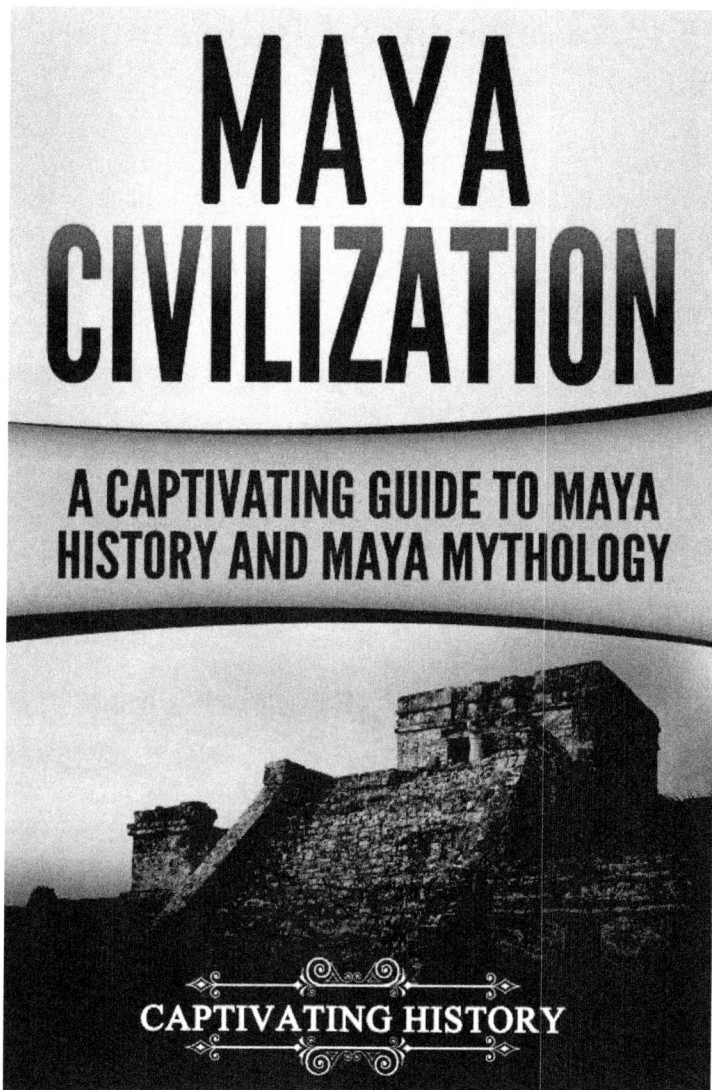

MAYA CIVILIZATION

A CAPTIVATING GUIDE TO MAYA HISTORY AND MAYA MYTHOLOGY

CAPTIVATING HISTORY

Free Bonus from Captivating History (Available for a Limited time)

Hi History Lovers!

Now you have a chance to join our exclusive history list so you can get your first history ebook for free as well as discounts and a potential to get more history books for free! Simply visit the link below to join.

Captivatinghistory.com/ebook

Also, make sure to follow us on:

Twitter: @Captivhistory

Facebook: Captivating History:@captivatinghistory

Printed in Great Britain
by Amazon

55048568R00046